READ ABOUT
Reptiles

Jen Green

COPPER BEECH BOOKS
BROOKFIELD • CONNECTICUT

Contents

© Aladdin Books Ltd 2000

Designed and produced by
Aladdin Books Ltd
28 Percy Street
London W1P 0LD

First published in
the United States in 2000 by
Copper Beech Books,
an imprint of
The Millbrook Press
2 Old New Milford Road
Brookfield, Connecticut 06804

ISBN 0-7613-1214-5

Cataloging-in-Publication data is on
file at the Library of Congress.

Printed in U.A.E.

All rights reserved

Editor
Sarah Milan

Series Editor
Jim Pipe

Science Consultant
David Burnie

Series Literacy Consultant
Wendy Cobb

Design
Flick, Book Design and Graphics

Picture Research
Brooks Krikler Research

What Are Reptiles?

A reptile is a kind of animal. Unlike us, reptiles have lived on Earth for millions of years. One group of reptiles that lived on our planet millions of years ago was the dinosaurs.

Others, like lizards, tortoises, and crocodiles, are all types of reptile that still live today.

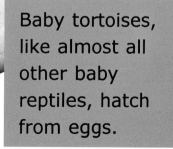

Baby tortoises, like almost all other baby reptiles, hatch from eggs.

Scientists have put reptiles into four groups —
snakes and lizards, the crocodile family, turtles
and tortoises, and a reptile called the tuatara.

This snake, the puff adder, lives all over Africa,
except in deserts and on mountain tops.

Reptiles live in most places, except where it
is very cold. They are found both on dry land
and in water. Some live in harsh places such
as hot, dry deserts and rocky mountains.

Snakes, lizards, tortoises, and crocodiles all look very different from each other. They have certain things in common, though. It is these things that make them reptiles.

Reptiles are cold-blooded, which means they need to lie in the sun to warm up. They have a dry, scaly skin and lungs that breathe air. Inside their body is a skeleton of bones. Almost all reptiles hatch from eggs.

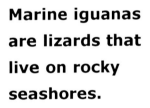

Marine iguanas are lizards that live on rocky seashores.

A snake's scales

Have you ever touched a snake or a lizard? Reptiles feel dry and cool to touch, not wet and clammy like frogs.

A reptile's skin is made up of scales. They overlap like tiles on a roof. The skin between them is flexible so the reptile can move about. This tough cover protects a reptile from danger.

Most reptiles shed their scales in patches. Snakes shed their skin all at once. This is called sloughing.

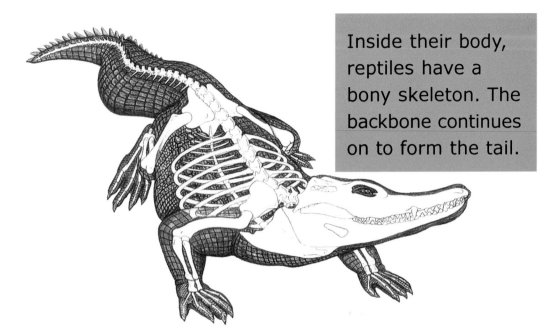

Inside their body, reptiles have a bony skeleton. The backbone continues on to form the tail.

There are about 6,500 different species (kinds) of reptiles living in the world today. Most of them are lizards or snakes.

A very special reptile lives on the islands of New Zealand. The tuatara is the only surviving member of a family of reptiles that lived on Earth at the same time as the dinosaurs.

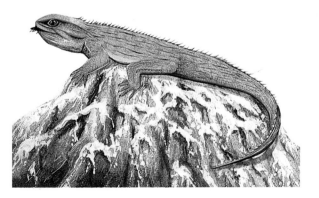

How Reptiles Live

You read earlier that reptiles are "cold-blooded." This doesn't mean their body is always cold. In fact, reptiles are usually as warm or cold as the air or water around them.

They need heat from the sun to make them warm. This means that reptiles use up little energy to keep warm, so they need less food.

Like all reptiles, this collared lizard warms up by lying in the sun. To cool down, it moves into the shade.

At dawn, the lizard comes out to soak up the warmth of the sun.

At midday, the lizard cools in the shade.

In the evening, it catches the last rays of the sun.

At night, the lizard returns to its safe, warm burrow.

Many reptiles spend a lot of the day moving from a cool place to a warm one and back again. This keeps their body at the right temperature.

Tortoises are kept as pets in cold countries. In winter, they must be put in a safe and warm place.

Reptiles in cold countries spend all winter in a deep sleep. They only wake up when it's spring. This is called hibernation.

Most reptiles are meat-eaters. Snakes and crocodiles hunt for food. Giant lizards called Komodo dragons feed mainly on dead animals.

Reptiles often snap up their prey alive and swallow it whole because their teeth aren't very good at chewing or crushing food.

The slow-moving tortoise eats plants. It can't move fast enough to hunt for food!

A snake can't chew, so it swallows its food whole.

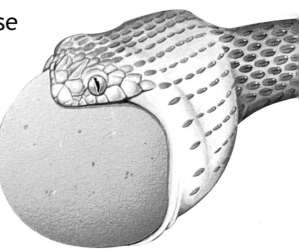

The chameleon is a type of lizard. It feeds on insects, which it catches with its long, sticky tongue.

After they hatch, baby turtles make their way to the sea.

Most baby reptiles hatch out from eggs that their mother lays after mating. She lays them in the sand or soil, or under rocks. The babies are protected by the egg's tough shell.

Tortoises, crocodiles, and alligators lay eggs with hard shells like birds' eggs. Snakes, turtles, and most lizards lay eggs with soft, leathery shells.

Reptile babies look like a small version of their parents. Most reptile parents don't take care of their young after they hatch. The babies are left to look after themselves.

There are a few reptiles that do not hatch from eggs. Some snakes and lizards grow inside their mother's body instead.

Unlike other reptiles, the mother crocodile looks after her babies. Here, she carries them carefully in her mouth to the water's edge.

13

Slithering Snakes

How Snakes Move • Senses • Hunting

Snakes are long, legless reptiles. Did you know that there are 2,400 different kinds of snakes? The largest — giant pythons — grow up to thirty feet long.

Snakes get around very well without legs. They loop their body into curves. The curves press against the ground to push the snake along.

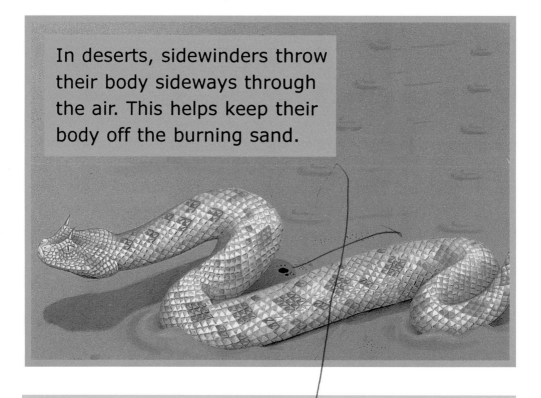

In deserts, sidewinders throw their body sideways through the air. This helps keep their body off the burning sand.

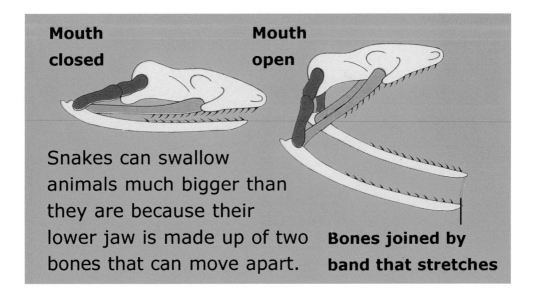

Mouth closed

Mouth open

Snakes can swallow animals much bigger than they are because their lower jaw is made up of two bones that can move apart.

Bones joined by band that stretches

Snakes have no ears. They "hear" by picking up sounds as they travel through the ground.

Some snakes have special senses. Pit vipers have little pits (sunken areas) in their cheeks that can sense heat from animals. This means they can hunt them even when it's dark.

Snakes flick out their tongue to collect faint scents in the air. They can then "taste" the scents.

Pythons and boa constrictors wrap their body around their victim, squeezing it to death.

Snakes are meat-eaters, or carnivores. They hunt birds, lizards, and furry mammals, and they also steal animals' eggs.

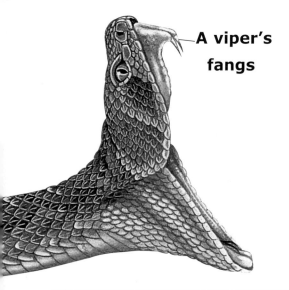

A viper's fangs

Snakes have different ways of killing their prey. Some snakes are poisonous. Cobras, vipers, and rattlesnakes bite their prey with their long, curving teeth, called fangs.

Most snakes aren't harmful. Of the 2,400 different species of snake around the world, only about 400 have poison that is strong enough to harm other animals.

This snake has a tail that "rattles" when it is shaken. Do you know which snake it is? Answer on page 32.

Hollow tail pieces

All Kinds of Lizards

Size and Shape • Getting Around • Escaping Danger

Lizards are the largest group of reptiles. There are over 3,700 different kinds. The smallest is a tiny gecko less than two inches long. The biggest is the Komodo dragon, ten feet long.

Lizards live mainly in warm countries. They are welcome in many people's homes because they eat flies and other insects.

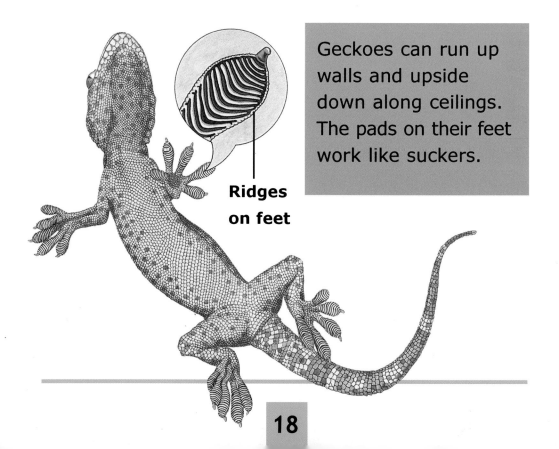

Ridges on feet

Geckoes can run up walls and upside down along ceilings. The pads on their feet work like suckers.

18

The flying gecko has flaps of loose skin. These work like a parachute as the lizard glides from the treetops.

Most lizards look like this jeweled lacerta lizard — they have a big head, a slim body, and a long tail. But some lizards that burrow in soil have no legs, and look more like snakes.

There are only two poisonous lizards — the Gila monster and the Mexican beaded lizard. They live in the deserts of North America.

Jeweled lacerta lizard

19

Lizards protect themselves from danger in different ways.

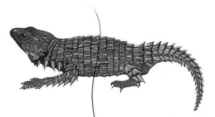

The armadillo lizard is covered in spikes.

Many have a brown or green body that blends in with the ground or leaves, so they can hide from danger. This is called camouflage.

A chameleon can change its skin color in seconds to match its surroundings.

When an enemy comes near, it rolls itself into a ball.

This Nile monitor lizard grows up to six feet long. It digs, runs, and swims well, and can also climb trees.

This lizard uses a clever trick to escape birds. Can you see how it escapes? The answer is on page 32.

Other lizards frighten enemies away by swelling up, hissing, and lashing their tail. The Australian frilled lizard spreads out its large collar to warn off attackers.

What is this gecko hiding against? Answer on page 32.

A crocodile pounces on a wildebeest crossing a river. It will drag the wildebeest underwater until it drowns.

The Crocodile Family

Types of Crocodilian • Hunting • Swimming

Crocodiles and alligators both belong to the crocodile family — a group known as crocodilians. The crocodile family also includes caimans and gavials.

Caiman

Alligator

Caimans have a short snout. Gavials have long, thin jaws filled with sharp teeth.

Gavial

Crocodiles are deadly hunters. Their main weapons are their big jaws and needle-sharp teeth.

The gavial's name comes from a word for "pot." Can you guess why? The answer is on page 32.

Alligators look similar to crocodiles. But they have a broader head and only their upper teeth show when their mouth is closed. They are not such fierce hunters as crocodiles.

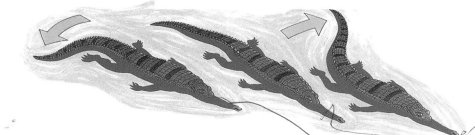

A crocodile moves through the water by moving its strong tail from side to side.

Crocodiles can live for 100 years, slowly growing larger and larger. On land, they lumber along on their short legs, but in the water, they are fast, strong swimmers.

Tortoises and Turtles

Tortoises and turtles are famous for the hard, heavy shell that covers their body. This protects them just like a suit of armor.

When an enemy comes near, they don't need to run away. Instead, they pull their head and legs inside their shell.

Shell ————

A tortoise's shell is made of about sixty bony plates joined together. The plates are covered with a horny or leathery covering.

Turtles spend almost all their life at sea. Their front feet are shaped like paddles to help them swim.

The tortoise family includes terrapins and turtles. Terrapins live in rivers and ponds. Turtles swim far out at sea.

Female turtles come ashore to have their young. They lay their eggs in a hole in the sand. When the babies hatch, they dig themselves out and scurry down to the water before they are eaten by birds or crabs.

Terrapin

Tortoises live on land in many different places, from rain forests to deserts. They move very slowly, weighed down by their load. Try taking just one small step every two seconds. That's how slowly a tortoise moves.

Tortoises are too slow to catch other animals for food, and they eat mainly plants. They don't have teeth, so they crunch up their food with their hard, horny jaws.

The snapping turtle has a tongue shaped like a worm. It uses this as bait to catch passing fish. When a fish swims up to eat the "worm," the turtle quickly snaps it up.

Reptiles of the Past

From Sea to Land • Dinosaurs • Dying Out

The first reptiles appeared on Earth about 350 million years ago. They developed from animals that had crawled out of the sea to live partly on land and partly in the water.

Before reptiles, all animals laid their eggs in water. But reptiles' eggs had a special shell that stopped them from drying out. So a reptile mother could lay her eggs on dry land.

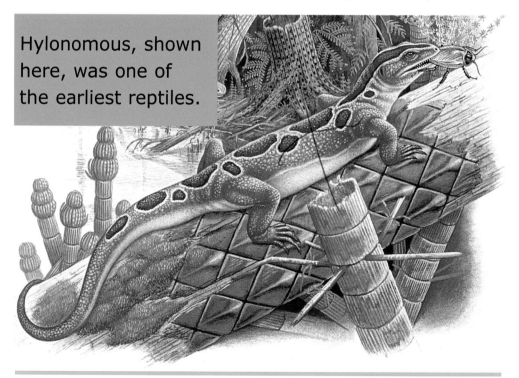

Hylonomous, shown here, was one of the earliest reptiles.

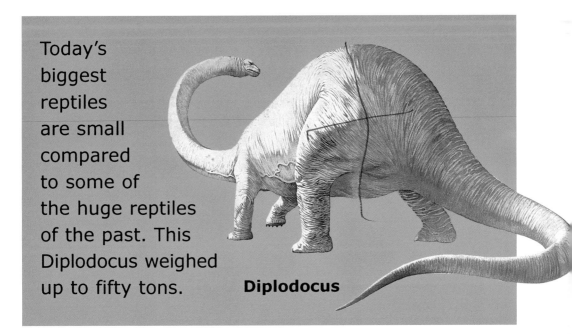

Today's biggest reptiles are small compared to some of the huge reptiles of the past. This Diplodocus weighed up to fifty tons.

Diplodocus

Once free of the water, reptiles developed better ways of breathing and moving on land. For the next 200 million years, they were the most successful group of animals on Earth.

But about sixty-five million years ago, most reptiles, including the dinosaurs, died out. They may have been killed by a giant meteor.

Only four groups of reptiles — snakes and lizards, tortoises and turtles, the crocodile family, and the tuatara — still live on today.

Find Out More

PICTURE QUIZ

Do you know which of the following animals are reptiles and which are not? The answers are on page 32.

Frog   **Snail**   **Turtle**   **Lizard**

UNUSUAL WORDS

Here we explain some of the words you have read in this book.

Camouflage This is when an animal hides from danger by blending in with its surroundings.

Carnivore An animal that eats mainly meat.

Cold-blooded Used to describe reptiles and other animals that need heat from the sun to warm their body.

Constrictor A type of snake that kills its prey by squeezing it to death.

Fangs The long, pointed teeth of some snakes.

Hatch When a baby reptile or bird hatches, it breaks out of its shell.

Hibernate An animal hibernates when it sleeps all winter to save energy in cold weather.

Prey An animal that is hunted for food.

Scales The thick patches of skin that cover a reptile's body.

Slough When a snake sloughs, it sheds its skin all at once.

Species A particular type of animal or plant. The Nile crocodile is a species of reptile.

Tuatara A rare reptile that lives only in New Zealand. It belongs to a reptile group of its own.

RECORD BREAKERS

Biggest Reptile

Saltwater crocodiles are the largest living reptiles. The biggest grow as heavy as a ton. The longer they live, the larger they grow!

Saltwater crocodile

Fastest Reptile

Spiny-tailed iguanas are the world's fastest lizards. They can race along at up to twenty-two mph.

THE ANIMAL KINGDOM

Scientists have put animals into groups to show how they are related. Reptiles are closest to amphibians.

ANIMALS WITH BACKBONES

Mammals	Birds	Reptiles	Amphibians	Fish

ANIMALS WITHOUT BACKBONES

MOLLUSKS

Snails	Clams	Octopuses

ARTHROPODS

Spiders	Insects	Crustaceans

PRIMITIVE ANIMALS

SINGLE-CELL ANIMALS	SPONGES
STARFISH	JELLYFISH
WORMS	

31

Index

ANSWERS TO PICTURE QUESTIONS

Page 17 This is a rattlesnake.
Page 21 (top) The lizard's tail breaks off in the bird's mouth. The lizard escapes and, in time, it grows back a new tail.
Page 21 (bottom) The gecko is hiding against tree bark.

Page 24 Male gavials have a mound on the end of their nose that looks like a small pot.
Page 30 The turtle and the lizard are both reptiles. The frog is an amphibian and the snail is a mollusk.

Photocredits: Cover and pages 16, 21, 22 & 27—Oxford Scientific Films. 1, 2 & 4—John Foxx Images.
3, 8, 10-11 & 12—Bruce Coleman Collection. 6 & 23—Digital Stock. 26—Jacques le Pipe.
Illustrators: Tessa Barwick, Dave Burroughs, James Field, Gary Hinks, Alan Male, Phil Weare, David Wood.